Psychopathology And Religion

J. Cyril Flower

Kessinger Publishing's Rare Reprints

Thousands of Scarce and Hard-to-Find Books
on These and other Subjects!

- Americana
- Ancient Mysteries
- Animals
- Anthropology
- Architecture
- Arts
- Astrology
- Bibliographies
- Biographies & Memoirs
- Body, Mind & Spirit
- Business & Investing
- Children & Young Adult
- Collectibles
- Comparative Religions
- Crafts & Hobbies
- Earth Sciences
- Education
- Ephemera
- Fiction
- Folklore
- Geography
- Health & Diet
- History
- Hobbies & Leisure
- Humor
- Illustrated Books
- Language & Culture
- Law
- Life Sciences
- Literature
- Medicine & Pharmacy
- Metaphysical
- Music
- Mystery & Crime
- Mythology
- Natural History
- Outdoor & Nature
- Philosophy
- Poetry
- Political Science
- Science
- Psychiatry & Psychology
- Reference
- Religion & Spiritualism
- Rhetoric
- Sacred Books
- Science Fiction
- Science & Technology
- Self-Help
- Social Sciences
- Symbolism
- Theatre & Drama
- Theology
- Travel & Explorations
- War & Military
- Women
- Yoga
- *Plus Much More!*

We kindly invite you to view our catalog list at:
http://www.kessinger.net

VII

PSYCHOPATHOLOGY AND RELIGION

In discussing the relation of analytical psychology to poetic art, C. G. Jung laid down the following important principle :

> ' . . . *only that portion of art which consists in the process of artistic form can be an object of psychology, but that which constitutes the essential nature of art must always lie outside its province. This other portion, namely, the problem what is art in itself, can never be the object of a psychological, but only of an aesthetico-artistic method of approach.*
>
> ' A similar distinction must also be made in the realm of religion ; there also a psychological consideration is permissible only in respect of the emotional and symbolical phenomena of a religion, wherein the essential nature of religion is in no way involved, as indeed it cannot be. For were this possible, not religion alone, but art also could be treated as a mere subdivision of psychology. In saying this I do not mean to affirm that such an encroachment has not actually taken place '.[1]

In another place Jung writes :

> ' To our analytical psychology, which from the human standpoint must be regarded as an empirical science, the image of God is the symbolic expression of a certain psychological state, or function. . . .
>
> ' . . . God is not even relative, but a function of the unconscious, namely the manifestation of a split-off sum of libido, which has activated the God-*imago* '.[2]

In the light of this it becomes a pertinent question whether Jung himself has not been guilty of the encroachment he describes and condemns. A further examination of typical references to the religious problem in his writings tends to confirm the suspicion that Jung not only claims the right

---

[1] Paper, *On the Relation of Analytic Psychology to Poetic Art*, British Journal of Medical Psychology, vol. III., Part III., p. 213.

[2] *Psychological Types*, 1923, pp. 300, 301.

to examine the beliefs and symbols of religion as subjective fabrications, which is perfectly legitimate and necessary, but passes on to philosophical and theological conclusions of a negative character, which could only be established, or refuted, by epistemological and theological discussion. Already in an earlier volume Jung advances the thesis that the essence of religion is bound up with the sexual life.

> ' . . . *in essence our life's fate is identical with the fate of our sexuality*. If Freud and his school devote themselves first and foremost to tracing out the individual's sexuality it is certainly not in order to excite piquant sensations, but to gain a deeper insight into the driving forces that determine that individual's fate. In this we are not saying too much, rather understating the case. If we can strip off the veils shrouding the problems of individual destiny, we can afterwards widen our view from the history of the individual to the history of nations. And first of all we can look at the history of religions, at the history of the phantasy-systems of whole peoples and epochs. The religion of the Old Testament elevated the *paterfamilias* to the Jehovah of the Jews whom the people had to obey in fear and dread. The Patriarchs are an intermediate stage towards the deity. The neurotic fear and dread of the Jewish religion, the imperfect, not to say unsuccessful attempt at the sublimation of a still too barbarous people, gave rise to the excessive severity of the Mosaic Law, the ceremonial constraint of the neurotic '.[1]

That there was ' fear and dread ' in Jewish religion no-one would deny ; nor the further fact that elements of fear and dread are present at all times in first-hand religion ; but on what ground is the fear and dread labelled ' neurotic ' ? The assumption is that the fear and dread were ' false ' in the sense that phobias and obsessions are false. But psychology is not in a position to give judgment on this issue, on Jung's own showing. It is an encroachment of psychopathology on the realm of philosophy and theology. Nor is this an isolated encroachment on the part of Jung's

---

[1] *Collected Papers on Analytical Psychology*, 2nd edn., 1917, p. 172.

psychology. In the *Psychology of the Unconscious* a
further step is taken towards the elaboration of a dogma
of the pure subjectivity of religion. We are told :

> ' Just as psychoanalysis in the hands of the physician, a secular
> method, sets up the real object of transference as the one to take
> over the conflicts of the oppressed and to solve them, so the
> Christian religion sets up the Saviour, considered as real. . . .
> One must not forget that the individual psychologic roots of the
> Deity, set up as real by the pious, are concealed from him, and
> that he, although unaware of this, still bears the burden alone
> and is still alone with his conflict. This delusion would lead
> infallibly to the speedy breaking up of the system, for Nature
> cannot indefinitely be deceived, but the powerful institution of
> Christianity meets this situation. . . . The Deity continues to
> be efficacious in the Christian religion only upon the foundation
> of brotherly love '.[1]

This leads on to the assertion that in these days the work
of Christianity has really been done :

> ' The Christian religion seems to have fulfilled its great bio-
> logical purpose, in so far as we are able to judge. It has led
> human thought to independence, and has lost its significance,
> therefore, to a yet undetermined extent '.[2]

The way it has achieved this has been by effecting repressions which safeguard humanity against a dissoluteness in
which it could not thrive[3]. We no longer understand
the ' feeling of redemption ' which it brought, protected
as we are by barriers of its making.

> ' Most certainly we should still understand it, had our customs
> even a breath of ancient brutality, for we can hardly realise in
> this day the whirlwinds of the unchained libido which roared
> through the ancient Rome of the Cæsars. The civilized man of
> the present day seems very far removed from that. He has
> become merely neurotic. So for us the necessities which brought
> forth Christianity have actually been lost, since we no longer
> understand their meaning. We do not know against what it had
> to protect us. For enlightened people, the so-called religiousness
> has already approached very close to a neurosis. In the past

---

[1] *Psychology of the Unconscious*, pp. 75, 76.
[2] *Op. cit.*, p. 85.   [3] *Op. cit.*, p. 79.

two thousand years Christianity has done its work and has erected barriers of repression, which protect us from the sight of our own " sinfulness " '.[1]

The implication of this teaching seems quite clearly to be that religion is a device for transference of a peculiarly subjective sort. Ideas are fabricated or accepted which bear no relation to the real elements in the situation, and by virtue of the completely mistaken belief in their validity helpful adaptation is made to the real situation. Since this device relates man to no reality beyond himself and his appetites, when once it has succeeded in its ' biological function ', of setting a limit to the ' unchained libido ', it ceases to have any validity, and its cultivation is by way of being neurotic. Surely this again is an ' encroachment ' on the part of Jung's particular psychology into the domain of what religion essentially is. The discovery of the modes of operation of mental mechanisms involved in the religious response is not the same thing as the discovery of what it is that the response is answering. The psychology of religion has no criterion by which to test the validity of the outer or objective reference of mental processes, and nothing is proved one way or the other by the recognition that mechanisms of ' projection ', for example, are involved in religion. They are no less involved, in one form or another, in most of the characteristic psychological processes. What used to be called ' sensation ' in the static psychology of the past, is now described as ' sensory response '—which involves the recognition of the inner activity initiated by the stimulus, and when we come to the perceptual response, the element of projection is quite definite. Perceptual response means the endowment of a

[1] *Op. cit.*, p. 80.

group or system of stimuli with numerous characteristics which they obviously have not got in themselves. It not only interprets the stimuli, and projects the interpretation on the ' external world ', but it readily projects upon partial stimulation an overplus of interpretation, a point clearly brought out by Dr. Dawes Hicks in a recent article :

' . . . our perception tends to become less and less dependent upon what, at the time, is actually given ; we bring to bear upon what is given a wealth of awareness which ensures that no perceptive act is ever, even in its incipient stage, devoid of specific content. Furthermore, it is precisely this wealth of accumulated awareness that constitutes what we are in the habit of describing as our experience ; and in a very real sense it can be said that it is its experience which *makes* a mind '.[1]

But we are not justified on psychological grounds in asserting that therefore the *esse* of a thing is its *percipi*. In the same way, to shew that the mechanisms of projection, transference, etc., are at work in the religious response does not warrant any conclusion, positive or negative, about the existence or nature of the objective reference of religion.

It is to be noted that Jung's illicit conversion of psychology into quasi-theology is largely dominated by the fallacy to which Rivers has drawn attention[2], and which is a particular instance of the fallacy of rationalization. This fallacy becomes explicit in the passage purporting to explain why Christianity was originally accepted :

' At this time, when a large part of mankind is beginning to discard Christianity, it is worth while to understand clearly why it was originally accepted. It was accepted in order to escape

[1] *On the Nature of Images*, British Journal of Psychology, vol. XV., Part 2, p. 130.
[2] ' One of the fundamental fallacies of the anthropologist . . . is to suppose that because a rite or other institution fulfils a certain utilitarian purpose, it therefore came into being in order to fulfil that purpose.' Quoted above, p. 8.

at last from the brutality of antiquity. As soon as we discard it, licentiousness returns, as impressively exemplified by life in our large modern cities '.[1]

Christianity was accepted because in a number of quite unforeseen and unthought of ways, it actually provided mankind with a firmer foothold in a growingly mysterious world. It provided means of release and expression for activities which would otherwise have been baffled. In fact, the truer way of stating the case would be to say that men and women found through Christian ideas and practices a mode of response which brought harmony into life, and this was the process of accepting Christianity. That it also enabled man ' to escape from the brutality of antiquity ' is not questioned, but that this was the motive for their acceptance of it is psychologically improbable to the last degree. Jung is confusing effects achieved with intentions. No mere recognition of the social dangers of licentiousness is capable of eliciting of itself a religious response, nor of persuading mankind to adopt religious beliefs and behaviour recommended to it as an antidote to such evils. God could never have been ' invented ', nor a religious system, such as Christianity, accepted, as the result of conscious recognition of utility. Something brings man to the experience of his own inadequacy, and that something that is ' other ' and ' beyond,' usually gets formulated in the end as ' God ' (the exception being early Buddhism). But in all this there is no purposive striving towards ends of great biological utility. How entirely this fundamental psychological character of the religious response escapes Jung, seems to me to be indicated in the following passage :

[1] *Psychology of the Unconscious*, p. 258.

' I think *belief should be replaced by understanding ;* then we should keep the beauty of the symbol, but still remain free from the depressing results of submission to belief. This would be the psychoanalytic cure for belief and disbelief '.[1]

The essence of religion, psychologically, is the impingement upon human consciousness of that which cannot be understood. What can be understood passes into the heritage of knowledge, and ceases to be impregnated with the emotions that surround the mysterious. Such an extension of the realm of ' understanding ' is constantly proceeding, as I have already maintained ; but its very process involves an ever-deepening awareness of the mysterious immensity, the intellectually baffling ocean of the uncharted ' beyond ' in which all appearances float. As Prof. L. T. Hobhouse has said, reason

' insists as a first principle on the relativity of all human conceptions, on the narrowness of the area reclaimed by knowledge as compared with the ocean of reality, and on the unlimited power of human capacity to expand and explore. . . . We stand on the edge of illimitable, unexplored regions, into which our vision penetrates but a little way. But at least we can dismiss as foolish the fear that science will exhaust the interest of reality, or peace destroy the excitement of life, or the reign of reason cramp imagination. The conquests of mind have a very different effect. The more territory that it brings under its sway, the vaster the unconquered world looms beyond '.[2]

It is always with this vaster unconquered world that looms beyond that religion is concerned, particularly in its manifold relations with that world which has been brought under the sway of reason. Consequently, it is impossible in *religion* to substitute understanding for belief. Religious belief, which can be fully and adequately expressed in terms of scientific understanding, ceases to be religious.

[1] *Op. cit.,* p. 263.
[2] *Morals in Evolution*, 2nd ed., 1908, vol. II., pp. 256-7.

We believe religiously precisely where we cannot understand scientifically. The problem of freeing man from the depressing results of submission to dogmatic belief is a very real one, but its solution does not involve the elimination of belief any more than the solution of the problem of a headache involves decapitation.

Jung's use of the expression ' the psychoanalytic cure for belief and disbelief ' leads on to a point of view with regard to religion which has gained considerable ground : the point of view, namely, which regards it as essentially something to be cured. Reference has already been made to the idea of religion as a psycho-neurosis[1], but a more detailed and critical examination of this point of view will throw light upon the value and the limitations of the contribution of psychopathology to the psychological problems of religion, and at the same time may afford further evidence, or provide further illustration of the thesis here maintained. I propose, therefore, to consider the attempt of Everett Dean Martin, in a recently published volume, to give a systematic interpretation of religion in terms of psychopathology.[2]

Dismissing the methods of introspection and of behaviourism, Mr. Martin proposes to follow a third method in investigating the ' mystery of religion ', which is

' that of psychopathology. This method is primarily concerned with the study of abnormal types of behaviour, but it throws much light upon the psychic life of normal people. There need be nothing startling in the proposal to study religion as a psychopathic phenomenon. Starbuck and James carried the study into this field years ago, although their work was done before general psychology possessed the analytic method of Freud '.[3]

[1] See above, pp. 42-45.   [2] *The Mystery of Religion*, 1924.
[3] *Op. cit.*, p. 47.

It may be well at this point to recall the concluding passages of James's Lecture on Religion and Neurology, lest it should be supposed that his attitude was the same as that of Martin :

> ' As regards the psychopathic origin (James writes) of so many religious phenomena, that would not be in the least surprising or disconcerting, even were such phenomena certified from on high to be the most precious of human experiences. No one organism can possibly yield to its owner the whole body of truth. Few of us are not in some way infirm, or even diseased ; and our very infirmities help us unexpectedly. In the psychopathic temperament we have the emotionality which is the *sine qua non* of moral perception ; we have the intensity and tendency to emphasis which are the essence of practical moral vigor ; and we have the love of metaphysics and mysticism which carry one's interests beyond the surface of the sensible world. What, then, is more natural than that this religious temperament should introduce one to regions of religious truth, to corners of the universe, which your robust Philistine type of nervous system, forever offering its biceps to be felt, thumping its breast, and thanking Heaven that it hasn't a single morbid fibre in its composition, would be sure to hide forever from its self-satisfied possessors ?
>
> ' If there were such a thing as inspiration from a higher realm, it might well be that the neurotic temperament would furnish the chief condition of the requisite receptivity. And having said thus much, I think that I may let the matter of religion and neuroticism drop '.[1]

What Martin actually intends in his application of the method of psychopathology may be gathered from the following two quite representative quotations :

> ' . . . what if religion were originally fabricated, and its " mysteries " cherished generation after generation, to be an *escape from the very reality* into which modernism would fain confine the objects of religious interest ! '[2]
>
> ' *Is it not possible that those unconscious psychic mechanisms which among unadjusted persons find expression in the neuroses, do, under other circumstances appear as religious behavior ?* Religion would appear from this point of view to be a sort of *beneficent psychosis*, or perhaps a socially acceptable substitute '.[3]

[1] *The Varieties of Religious Experience*, p. 24-5.
[2] *Op. cit.*, p. 10.   [3] *Op. cit.*, p. 56-7.

The ' real ' world is, according to admission, largely extra-rational, and all thinking about it is symbolic—scientific thinking no less than religious and artistic :

> ' As to scientific ideas, their symbolic nature is recognizable when we remember that the " laws " and class concepts of science are really " shorthand " devices, signs by which we are able to indicate that a group of phenomena are similar in a certain respect'.[1]

Nevertheless we are to understand that ' reality ' is too harsh and uncomfortable for man to accept and adapt himself to, and accordingly he distorts it, or ignores it, or accepts substitutes for it, by projecting from the un-conscious all kinds of fancies, which roughly represent ' our wish that the universe were run in our interest'.[2] Accordingly, religion is precisely the escape from reality to which reference has already been made. Mr. Martin is very insistent on this point, again and again affirming that the real nature of religion is not that it adapts man to his environment, but that it takes him out of his ' real ' environment, provides him with a means of escape.[3]

But at this point a perplexing problem arises which the author seems entirely to have overlooked. From what ' real ' world is religion a means of escape ? Is it the world of ' everyday experience ' ? But the world of everyday experience is, on his own shewing, steeped, no less than the world of religious experience, in symbolism.[4] Accordingly I must enter a protest against the *petitio principii* in-volved in speaking of one world of experience as ' real '

---

[1] *Op. cit.*, p. 33.   [2] *Op. cit.*, p. 99.

[3] A brief criticism of the ' escape from reality ' theory of religion will be found in my *Psychological Studies of Religious Questions*, pp. 65-8.

[4] Martin gives as instances the use of the map and of the flag as country symbols. ' . . . by the use of the map we are able to *orient ourselves practically* to the reality which we call the United States of America ' (p. 35). ' The flag *orients* us *emotionally* to America ' (p. 36).

and another as not 'real' unless some criterion of a specific kind is offered. The only attempt to offer such a criterion is where religion is described as 'nonadaptive' behaviour. But to what is it 'nonadaptive'? There can be only one answer: it is nonadaptive to the realm in relation to which scientific and practical symbolism is adaptive. But it is not necessarily nonadaptive in relation to a realm which the religious person regards as being no less, but perhaps rather more real. The important fact is that the fantasies projected by religion are not mere escapes from a 'reality' which is displeasing: they are constructions around a reality which is baffling. Here again the difference between science and religion presents itself. Both are constructions around reality. They differ in the measure and the nature of the control they give. Science is that construction which gives control—using the term in a broad sense to include the power to foretell. Only if the real is equated with the controllable can Mr. Martin's thesis stand. The religious man asserts that the uncontrollable, which he is constrained to endeavour to set forth in image and symbol, is just as real, though it defeats all his instinctive and habitual modes of response.

In the last chapter of the book, however, the emphasis is slightly altered; we are there told that:

'the real trouble is that people *cannot " stand themselves "* ' [1]

and that it is not so much the unpleasant or harsh nature of 'reality' as the inner turmoil which makes the religious haven of refuge a necessity. This, indeed, is the real

---

[1] *Op. cit.*, p. 379. ' . . . it is not at bottom the world of objects which people cannot stand. The real trouble is that people *cannot " stand themselves."* It is the struggle for self-appreciation which leads people to take refuge in a world of ideals.'

text around which the book is written. Man is regarded, religiously at least, as primarily an ' unconscious ' which is the arena of a conflict, because the unconscious is the product of impulses which have been inhibited, thus :

> ' During childhood the individual passes through a long and painful discipline in which he learns to inhibit certain impulses. The environment, he soon learns, necessarily leaves many of his desires unsatisfied. Conscious attention is soon diverted from these impulses and desires. Habits of thinking are cultivated which are in accord with what the environment requires. Thus these unattended tendencies to respond—many of them still being constantly stimulated from within the organism itself—drop out of consciousness. They become the " Unconscious " of psychopathology '.[1]

The mechanisms of religious experience and belief are accordingly exactly those of neurosis, psychosis and dreaming. In fact, it would seem that really it is the ' unconscious ' which ' cannot stand ' the conscious man and his orientation to experience, and it thus takes control, and all unknown to the man himself leads him to harbour images and to cherish ideas and to invent fictions which are simply substitute forms of wish fulfilment. So we find that the Œdipus complex figures as fundamental : a large part of religion is man's attempt to be reconciled with his father image :

> ' As the child approaches adolescence he begins to discover in himself the same force which his childish egoism led him to abolish from the image of the parents. He feels, therefore, that his own maturity is in conflict with the infantile father image through which he now adjusts himself to his world. In the attempt to solve this conflict we see a second and very important function of the father symbol—*the believer must be reconciled to the father* '.[2]

[1] *Op. cit.*, pp. 90-1. It is not clear whether Martin means to offer this as the account of the origin of the pathological unconscious, or as the origin of the unconscious which psychopathology has done so much to bring into the forefront of psychological discussion. In either case it is a very fragmentary and incomplete account.

[2] *Op. cit.*, p. 133.

But the mother symbol which appears to be omitted in the formulations of the Deity comes to its own in the religious community. The unconscious desire for the mother can receive symbolic satisfaction in the believer's union with the Church, which is ' mother ' :

> ' The church thus becomes the substitute for the object of that regressive love which would otherwise work serious injury to the psyche. It is consequently a means of grace, it is more than a delightful form of association among like-minded people. Membership in it completes the process of redemption. The symbolism which is used to express this feeling for the church is the language of the " Œdipus Complex " '.[1]

As an instance of the use of this language Mr. Martin actually records the fact that he read or heard that :

> ' a prominent clergyman left one of the large protestant communions a number of years ago, and at the time he left he gave utterance to certain " heretical " opinions in respect to the doctrine and discipline of the church in which he had been brought up. A professor in the leading theological school of the denomination issued a public denunciation of the apostate, saying that he had " slapped his mother in the face " '.[2]

The plausibility of the thoroughgoing psychoanalytic reduction of religion is largely due to the fact that a certain number of religious people suffer from conflicts and repressions which might have led to psycho-neurosis, but have found an outlet and a solution for their troubles in religious forms. The most casual observer of religious phenomena must have noticed how frequently religion has been the refuge of the emotionally thwarted and wounded.[3] Mr. Martin is not wrong in saying that religion

---

[1] *Op. cit.*, p. 241.   [2] *Op. cit.*, p. 239.

[3] In the course of a letter I received recently from a friend—of quite a general character, and not in response to any psychological question from me—she said : ' It seems to me, generally speaking, that the most religious people are the young who are on the verge of manhood and womanhood, and then in mature life, those who have failed adequately to satisfy the emotions in other ways and find what they need in religion and church life.'

is an escape, a consolation, and so forth, *in many instances*, but he is wrong in saying that it came into existence for that purpose, or that this is the essential mark of the religious response. There are psychasthenics in other walks of life beside religion ; but because a woman may find a symbolic satisfaction in nursing in a children's hospital it does not follow that children's hospitals came into existence in order to provide an outlet for the thwarted emotions and instincts of young women who could not otherwise solve their inner conflicts. There is much in Mr. Martin's book which is true and very suggestive Holy Mother Church may often enough be a refuge for the man who suffers from an infantile regression to the Œdipus phase ; but it does not follow that the image of mother was applied to the church because of this unconscious trend in those who founded it. On this ground we might as well say that men who, in later years, speak affectionately of their college or university as Alma Mater really went to college in order to gratify the unconscious incest wish, and that the notion that they went for the sake of education and fellowship was a pure rationalization.

What Mr. Martin succeeds in demonstrating in this book is that once religion had come into existence it probably saved the sanity and mental health of a large number of unstable persons, because they were able to find in it a means of resolving their unconscious conflicts—but, as Freud has shewn, the same may be true of almost any profession. To demonstrate that religion fulfills this, among other functions, is not to account psychologically for religion. The unstable person does not found a religion because he is unstable : he becomes neurotic or even psychotic unless there is something more than an instability which cannot 'stand' the world of everyday reality, or the self of everyday experience. The essential problem of the psychology of religion is those other factors, which provide the positive element in the religious response.

If it were not for his strong pathological bias Mr. Martin would probably have done more justice to facts and considerations which he mentions, but the significance of which he fails fully to appreciate, because they do not fit in with the pathological scheme. It will be instructive to consider some instances of this in which Mr. Martin seems to me to be stating premises, the conclusions of which can only be drawn in terms of the psychological account of religion, which it has been my aim to make some contribution towards outlining. Quite early in the first chapter we are told that :

> 'So large does the mysterious loom in religious experience that it is sometimes regarded as a basic reality in religion. It is said to be that which distinguishes faith from reason. Even so rationalistic a writer as Herbert Spencer seemed to feel that he was giving philosophic validity to the fundamental truth of religion when he maintained the existence of the unknowable, the eternal absolute, and inscrutable cosmic mystery.
>
> 'In very truth the cosmic mystery is ever about us. But I doubt if the mere philosophical fact that we do not and cannot know the ultimate is in itself enough to give rise to a religious appreciation of life'.[1]

But the cosmic mystery is not so easily dismissed as a 'mere philosophical fact'. It may be readily agreed that any philosophical doctrine about the cosmic mystery has little to do with giving rise to a religious appreciation of life ; but the mystery itself, in the concrete ways in which it emerges in various situations, is something very much more solid than a 'philosophical fact'. The mystery is,

[1] *Op. cit.*, p. 7.

in truth, an all-environing and unescapable fact, which only grows more and more insistent as man advances intellectually. This is, indeed, recognized elsewhere by Mr. Martin, when he says :

> ' Perhaps our nearest and truest approaches to reality are æsthetic. Irreducible to formula, the process which we call creation ever eludes the intellect and as pure thinkers we find ourselves in the end always with a mere form of thought. Yet that which we strive to grasp and understand is not an illusion. In it we live and move and have our being. The presence— which we can never escape—we are often aware of as a strange, yet indescribably intimate and immediate, fact of knowledge.
>
> Men have learned to call this mystery of our own and of all existence " God ". The words in which we speak of it matter little ; they are at best but attempts to communicate a fact which is unspeakable '.[1]

The mystery not only communicates itself as a fact in the experience of intellectual defeat, through which the wisest are ever brought to confess that the more we know, the less we understand about ultimate things, but it presses in on the practical and the emotional life no less :

> ' In one sense (Mr. Martin says), religion is a triumph of faith over pessimism. I believe this pessimism, even defeatism, is always at least unconsciously recognized by profoundly religious persons. Does not Christianity start with the doctrine that this is a lost world, redemption from which is promised through grace?' [2]

It is, indeed, on the practical side that the most impressive lessons of childhood are learned : while so many things can be imagined and thought, so few can be done because of the inexorable, mysterious and baffling limitations that hedge us in. More explicitly yet Mr. Martin seems to me in the last chapter to express precisely those facts of experience which support, not his psychopathic theory of religion, but the theory advanced in these pages. Speaking of the

---

[1] *Op. cit.*, p. 115.   [2] *Op. cit.*, pp. 64-5.

possibility of a ' revival of religion ', he enumerates a number of conditions which suggest its possibility, and among them this :

> ' There is obviously the fact of our industrialism. It was felt that the invention and use of power-driven machinery would lighten the burden of toil, and in a degree it has done so. But it has also created the modern industrial proletariat, a class of factory hands, gathered in our manufacturing centers not through any natural, mutual attraction on their part, but through the necessities of industry and the demand for labour. These people have been uprooted, torn out of their ancestral environment and are thrown into a mechanically organized world to which they are not adapted. Their old habits do not apply. Their labour processes have been depersonalized and standardized by the machine. . . .
>
> ' . . . All that is quaint, nonutilitarian, picturesque, fanciful, or unique, tends to fall behind and to perish. Human fellowship becomes an unstable equilibrium of forces. And in the degree that men see these forces for what they are, they are going to be unhappy. Labour to-day thinks that it is in revolt against capital. It is really in revolt against the thraldom of industrial processes which under any social system can mean only servitude for the great mass of mankind. As men become aware of this fact—and they must—is it unthinkable that they will seek compensation and escape in religion ? "[1]

I entirely agree that this describes conditions which are extremely likely to be the prelude to a religious ' revival ', but not primarily, because the conditions described are such as must be ' escaped ' from at the cost of a ' beneficent

---

[1] *Op. cit.*, pp. 350-2. It is interesting and instructive to compare the use made by Bertrand Russell in the passage referred to above, p. 181, of these conditions in his argument about the decay of religion. He considers that the chief reason for the decay of religion is the growth of an industrialism which removes men from close contact with irregularities, such as those of the weather. But his view of religion differs from that of Martin, as well as from that of this book. ' The whole of traditional religion,' he states on p. 47 (*Prospects of Industrial Civilization*) ' may be regarded as an attempt to mitigate the terror inspired by destructive natural forces.' ' The fact is that religion is no longer sufficiently vital to take hold of anything new ; it was formed long ago to suit certain ancient needs, and has subsisted by the force of tradition, but is no longer able to assimilate anything that cannot be viewed traditionally ' (p. 48). Russell—like so many others—is confusing religion with a very special form of religion.

psychosis ', but precisely because they are conditions which defeat existing equipment for response ; and the result of defeat must either be despair and collapse, or renewed effort in a fresh direction.   So far as men find themselves in a ' world to which they are not adapted ', and in which ' their old habits do not apply ', they either adapt themselves intelligently—if the conditions are such as lend themselves to practical understanding and control ; or, in other words, they utilize the plasticity of instinct and habit so as to redirect their activity and thought in such wise as to restore the lost equilibrium between self and environment ; or they must adapt themselves imaginatively if the situation cannot be brought into satisfactory relation with equipment.   Imaginative adaptation may take the form of art, but it is doubtful whether any artistic solution which is not also religious is possible for any but the few individuals who have special aptitudes for artistic expression.   A consciously ' make-believe ' compensation for a thwarting situation can be satisfactory to only the very few : most artists, and all art lovers who find help and joy in art appreciation feel that they are somehow being brought into relation with deeper reality which is ' beyond ' the access of reason, and would echo the words of Robert Browning :

' Sorrow is hard to bear, and doubt is slow to clear,
Each sufferer says his say, his scheme of the weal and woe :
But God has a few of us whom He whispers in the ear ;
The rest may reason and welcome : 'tis we musicians know '.[1]

---

[1] *Abt Vogler*, Stanza xi.   Both Mr. Bartlett, after reading the manuscript, and some of my students, after hearing the substance of this chapter in lecture form, raised the question of my view of the difference between art and religion.   I do not feel competent to speak with any authority on the psychology of art, nor is it necessary to my present purpose.   My point here is that religious experience is frequently expressed in the form of art, and that many artists, whether or not they use any conventional religious symbolism, display the essential marks of religion in their work.

From my point of view this is indistinguishable from religion. It involves precisely the same mechanisms, namely, the discrimination of baffling and ' beyond ' elements in the situation and the ' second-thought ' response to them through an imaginative interpretation which still feels them to be beyond intellectual understanding or control. If this imaginative work is wholly fantastic, and a mere ' escape ' from ' reality ', it is not, as I have already argued,[1] religious, but either pathological, or an adult substitute for fairy stories. But if it relates the situation to the equipment of those who have to face it, while inevitably leaving it essentially mysterious, and effectively directs the currents of activity in such ways as to secure the stability and psychological efficiency of the individual and the group, it is religious.

Again in the same chapter Mr. Martin observes :

' It is significant that each great mass movement in religion has followed a wave of intellectual advance, and has been the weapon used by the common man in his struggle against a situation which demanded of him too great a readjustment and thus made him feel unconsciously inferior. Christianity follows upon the heels of the Augustan age during which both at Rome and at Alexandria very rapid intellectual advance was being made. . . . The Reformation followed upon the Renaissance, the revival of learning which set Italy in the fifteenth century intellectually on fire and had begun to spread its light all over Europe. . . . English Puritanism also follows the brilliant Elizabethan age, and the " great revival " which appeared simultaneously in England and America at the close of the eighteenth century came as a reaction

I do not contend that all art is religion—a point I endeavoured to make clear on pages 140-142. The artistic response may be (i) a pure ' flight from reality,' offering relief and repose in an admittedly ' make-believe ' world ; (ii) an interpretation of ' reality ' aiming at enhancing its affective value ; (iii) a vision of ' reality ' environed in the unfathomable mystery. It is this third type of artistic response which I regard as being indistinguishable from religion.

[1] See above, pp. 42-5.

against what has been called the most mellow and like unto classic antiquity of all the Christian centuries, the century which spoke of itself as the " age of enlightenment " '.[1]

This relation between intellectual advance and the outburst of religion is precisely what we should expect if the main thesis of this book is correct. Intellectual advance is one part of the process of the fuller discrimination of the larger world, environed in mystery. Every extension of the kingdom of knowledge brings into clearer view the infinite ocean of that baffling mystery. What is to be done about it ? The philosopher may write about it in his intellectual terms, but the ordinary man, under the growing pressure of a universe which again and again defeats him alike practically and intellectually, gathers himself together and by the help of inner resources, fabricates the situation in such images as bring it within the realm of the familiar, trustworthy and friendly—as is illustrated in the case, already examined in some detail, of George Fox. That is the inevitable sequel to any period of advance in intellectual apprehension ; and judging by present day signs I should suggest that the religious revival which Mr. Martin fears is already in process, and that the revivalists are the scientists, who are ever coming upon the mysterious, the baffling, the utterly-beyond, in so various and impressive a fashion that in order to relate themselves to it they are compelled to fabricate it.

And here it will be appropriate to deal briefly with the question of the use of images and symbols. The psychoanalytic ' reduction ' method in religion assumes all the time that any term which is employed metaphorically is not only a symbol, but is a symbol for an unconscious wish,

[1] *Op. cit.*, pp. 370-1.

a repressed and probably discreditable element. Thus if we speak of ' Mother Church ', ' Father God ', etc., we must, according to this teaching, be unconsciously motivated, and any conscious valuation of the terms must be treated as pure rationalization. And the reason for this is, broadly, that in dealing with the psycho-neuroses analysts have found that the Œdipus complex is often if not always fundamental. But unless we assume, *ab initio* that religion is a pathological phenomenon, it is at least an equal chance that a metaphor may be a consciously chosen and employed metaphor as that it is primarily conditioned by repressed sexual or other instinctive motives. Mr. Martin quotes among other Old Testament passages, Hosea ii. 2-4 ; iv. 3-6 ; x. 13-14 ; xiii. 9 ; ii. 19, 20, 23, as illustrating the thesis that

> ' The Hebrews, conceiving of the community in terms of the mother image, " projected " upon the mother the sense of sin which they felt alienated them from the father '.[1]

This is a good instance of the bad habit of assuming that facts confirm a theory without adequately investigating the facts. We do not know, as a matter of fact, whether the story told by Hosea of his marrying ' a wife of whoredom ' is fact or fiction. A number of theories about the marriage have been held,[2] and it is just as possible that the prophet actually did marry a prostitute, and seek to reclaim her, as that the story is a parable. But whether it is experience or allegory, it still remains an unverified assumption that Hosea ' conceiving of the community in terms of the mother image ' is here ' projecting upon the mother the sense of sin ', etc., while the alternative hypothesis that

[1] *Op. cit.*, p. 229.
[2] Summarized in A. B. Davidson's Article on Hosea, Hastings' *Dictionary of the Bible*, vol. II., p. 421-2.

the prophet is making conscious use of a personal experience, or of his knowledge of another's experience, in loving and trying to reclaim a fallen woman, in interpreting the moral relationship between Yahweh and his faithless people is, to say the least of it, just as likely.   After all, a man's relationship with his wife is largely a conscious one, however much unconscious factors help to determine its character, and as conscious experience it provides manifold points of application to situations which are analogous.   For Hosea to depict the community as being like a faithless wife who is yet cared for, and sought with a redeeming love by Yahweh does not involve that he, or in general ' the Hebrews ', were suffering from an unresolved complex which had to issue in the ' beneficent psychosis ' of religion. It means simply that Hosea imaged the Deity as one whose relation to the people had essential points of similarity with that of a devotedly loving husband, whose love was not sexual appetite, but a redeeming passion.   And these images are applied to a Deity already formulated, and are in no sense the original projections which constituted the Hebrew conception of Yahweh.

That the sexual instinct and its components play a part, and a large part, in determining the imagery of religion no one would deny : the facts are patent.   Once the religious orientation is initiated, it inevitably employs in its work of specific formulation the native and acquired tendencies of man.   Thus the nutritive, the herd and the sex instincts all figure prominently in religious belief and practice.   Sir James G. Frazer's *Golden Bough* is an extended and detailed commentary upon religion as

' . . . the reverence or worship paid by men to the natural resources from which they draw their nutriment, both vegetable and animal. That they should invest these resources with an atmosphere of wonder and awe, often indeed with a halo of divinity, is no matter for surprise. The circle of human knowledge, illuminated by the pale cold light of reason, is so infinitesimally small, the dark regions of human ignorance which lie beyond that luminous ring are so immeasurably vast, that imagination is fain to step up to the border line and send the warm, richly coloured beams of her fairy lantern streaming out into the darkness ; and so, peering into the gloom, she is apt to mistake the shadowy reflections of her own figure for real beings moving in the abyss '.[1]

But he is careful to add that there is a great deal more in religion than this :

' . . . having said so much in this book of the misty glory which the human imagination sheds round the hard material realities of the food supply, I am unwilling to leave my readers under the impression, natural but erroneous, that man has created most of his gods out of his belly. That is not so, at least that is not my reading of the history of religion. Among the visible, tangible, perceptible elements by which he is surrounded—and it is only of these that I presume to speak—there are others than the merely nutritious which have exerted a powerful influence in touching his imagination and stimulating his energies, and so have contributed to build up the complex fabric of religion '.[2]

In particular Frazer proceeds to refer to the importance of the relations of the sexes to each other, and the influence of ' the forces of attraction by which mankind are bound together in society ' in the development of religion.

But although this is a wider recognition than that of some of the would-be interpreters of religion who see in it nothing but sublimation or distortion of herd instinct, sex instinct or self preservation instinct, it still remains a view which fails to give any account of what is really the main fact. Once religion as a special type of response has been initiated it naturally and inevitably deals with the major interests which man instinctively pursues, but the fundamental problem of religion is : How is it that man comes

[1] *The Golden Bough*, vol. VII., Pref., vii.
[2] *Op. cit.*, vol. VII., Pref., vii. and viii.

to pursue these interests no longer directly by instinctive and other controlled practical behaviour, but indirectly by fantasy, imagination, belief, etc. ? A careful scrutiny of the facts of the past, so far as these are available in reliable form, of the facts in connection with the behaviour and beliefs of modern ' primitives ', and of the essence of the processes of our own thought, seems to me to lead to this answer : It is because man is the animal which discriminates more than the isolated presentations for which there is adequate external stimulus, and he does this without having any specific mechanism inherent in his make-up for response. It is this fundamental fact—which itself cannot be explained at present by anything simpler—that lies behind all the mental conflicts, fantasies, daydreams, imaginations, visions, dreams, rationalizations, arts, philosophies, and religions of man. To attempt to derive religion from infantile mental processes is like trying to derive day from night. Infantile processes of fantasy and the rest are themselves the effects of contact with something which is more than the existing mechanisms for response are qualified to deal with. The fate of this ' over-response ' of fantasy depends on various factors and circumstances, which have been in some measure indicated. I may summarize thus : It may be (i) absolutely useless, futile, and non-adaptive. Any person actually trying to behave in relation to such a system would be classified as mentally deranged in any modern civilized community ; (ii) It may be practically effective, leading to symbolical formulations of ' reality ' which enable man more and more to control and to foretell ; (iii) It may be neither (i) nor (ii)—non-adaptive in the sense that it gives no definite control or power to foretell in relation to the mysterious element, but effective in that it liberates the activities, and directs them along channels of behaviour which on the whole do make for adaption to the larger world. The mystery or ' beyond ' is not reduced to nothing, but on the other hand it does not remain the source of mere psychic paralysis, collapse, or aberration. It is so fantasied, imagined and rationalized as to encourage man to continue his process of adaptation to a universe that perpetually baffles, and defeats, and consequently ever calls forth new recognition of the mystery, and further efforts to come to terms with it in imagination and rationalization.

This is the end of this publication.

Any remaining blank pages are for our book binding requirements and are blank on purpose.

To search thousands of interesting publications like this one, please remember to visit our website at:

http://www.kessinger.net

CPSIA information can be obtained at www.ICGtesting.com
Printed in the USA
BVOW081216231111

276806BV00007B/55/P